For my father, Nick Glumac,
the first poet I ever loved.

To Don,
In celebration
of your love of
nature. Ann

Contents

The Greening

Gone

After this long winter,
spring will come,
it will come.

Stubborn patches of snow
still hiding in shadows
will ease into cold, damp soil.

Buds will swell at the tips of branches,
though you won't see them.
You won't smell the first hint of green,
won't hear the peepers' evening choir.

After this long winter,
spring will come
but you won't be here
to feel the soft, easy wind,
the sun warming your back.

And after this long winter,
I don't care
if the grass turns green
or the robin sings.

Come She Will

Far in advance of the crocus' showy yellow,
the confident green of sun-warmed grass,
spring announces itself.

Faint perfume is teased from
tight-fisted buds suddenly visible
against a pale blue sky.

Musk rises up from patches of dirt
growing larger and closer together
amid the dirty snow.

Scents blend on the soft breeze
and you wait for her return.

Ice Storm

The spring nor'easter howled through the night.
We awake to a world cast in ice,
gray and white, color muffled by its thick layers.

Mighty pine trees are humbled by water, wind and cold,
their shoulders droop. They hold their limbs to the ground,
supplicants, palms up, seeking relief.

The Balm-o-Gilead creak and strain and shake off
the hard candy coating, sending down showers
on broken limbs scattered at their trunks.

Windows and grass, power lines and stop signs
are blurred and rimed and weighted,
transformed – and yet not –
by layers of powerful, ephemeral ice.

By afternoon, the thick frosting has melted,
the pines lift their dark green branches,
slowly, quietly.
The Balm-o-Gilead breathe out their healing scent,
branches with new-white scars,
limbs shining wet in the grass.

Spring Snow

The soft snow falls slowly,
hangs suspended over patches
of frozen earth.

In December, the flakes drifting
would be signal for cozy fires,
nights of reading and red wine,
skiing in brilliant sunshine.

Three days before April,
these pretty flakes are an insult, taken personally.
The snow whispers of the tyranny of winter,
the monochrome of days,
the unending cold and long, dark nights.

In the Balance

Throughout the night,
late April snow is thrown,
thick and heavy—
frosting brave new grass
and trees about to bud.
Thick enough to make a five-year-old squeal.

By morning,
Sugar Lake is cast in dull silver,
edged with poplars painted white.
A leaf—brown, curled—
hangs in the balance
between winter and summer.

April Morning

The pale green blade
arches up and out of cold soil,
stretching to catch
the soft rays of the sun,
just rising.

For months, it has been locked
in darkness, both
icy and complete.
It has dreamt
of dew drops catching
on its rough edges,
gentle winds dancing 'round
and the warm light
it reaches
with the palest and most slender
of tips.

The Greening

Slowly,
overnight
comes the greening.

New smells,
soft color
infuse the night air
and you know before you close the back door
it's here.

Dark hearts of winter,
teased out like buds on branches,
breathe deep
the greening.

Transubstantiation

Seasons

New-green leaves,
fluorescent in the horizontal morning light,
remind me time has passed.

Two winters have chilled and creaked
in the old house. Two springs have
breathed new life through the windows.

Maybe this summer won't seem so garish,
so full of life,
so achingly sweet.

Now that grief has receded,
its place taken
by simple longing,
maybe life won't seem so random
and unearned.

Lake Song

The loon cries out,
soft wail dancing along the lake,
flirting with the trees
that dip down over the shore.

In solitude
it calls out
and everyone,
everything, on shore
pauses for a split second
in appreciation
and recognition.

Questions About Trees

We know what makes leaves green,
the photosynthesis that performs
the alchemy,
transmuting water, sunlight, air
into an undulating mass.

But do we know what makes trees whisper
in soft evening breezes,
a susurrus as familiar and calming
as it is indecipherable?

Do we know how they dance
in summer storms?

Do we know why they choose
a particular moment to let go,
falling to earth,
settling into the soil?

Late May

A slow, tedious march toward spring
leaves me deadened to the changes –
pale, tentative leaves,
grass greening through the thatch,
birds busy building nests;
        they do not have the luxury
        of failing to notice
        longer days,
        southern breezes.

The spray of dandelions on a roadside
catches me,
holds me
in the wondrous, simple
beauty that is finally here,
that is spring.

Unwelcome

Weeds in the garden sprout
pale green against black-brown soil.
They do not know
they are unwelcome;
this is their existence—
to send roots out in search of food,
water,
to reach up through the heavy darkness
that is earth,
to find the light.

Common and useless, they live out their days,
growing, reproducing carelessly.
When pulled,
some give up
without a struggle,
tiny roots unearthed easily.

Others refuse, at first,
their taproots sunk deep,
deep into the ground.
They cling to the soil,
to life,
with a fierce tenacity
that suddenly gives way,
a gentle give,
a long exhale.

Red Fox Morning

Slipping in and out of long, dawn shadows
painted by a sun slowly rising,
the fox pads lightly through the wet field grass.

In and out of light and dark,
alternately glowing soft, muted red
or blending in with last year's grass,
he listens for the presence of field mice,
and, instead, senses my own.

He pauses only briefly
before continuing his search,
in and out of light and dark.

Where the aspen shimmer at field's edge,
twice he jumps high and dives
through the depths of light and dark
before padding back into the dark green of the woods.

Postcard

Hot, humid air presses down
on the rolling prairie,
condensing here to mist,
there to haze.

I-90 sidles up to cornfields,
beans
and rolls by proud houses
nestled in trees.

A lone sunflower
rooted on the side of the road
steadfastly faces east.

Sleeping Porch

Fading lilacs breathe a final, sweet perfume
through the screens,
filling the small porch
and resting on the sheets.

Fireflies dot the black field.
Peepers and crickets banter endlessly.

Warm, wet air is nudged about
by soft breezes
that cool me
as I sleep
on the porch
on a hot June night,
taking scent and sound and sight
to my bed
and to my dreams.

Superior

In the summer
on the Lake,
when the angle of the sun
stretches long,
when the green of leaves still holds the newness of spring,
there are many seasons.

In the morning,
your fingertips will touch
the cool of the night
held close to the earth;
your face will feel the warm breath
of a sun rising.

In the evening, breezes will whisper
over cold waters
and gather in cleft rocks
and cupped earth.
Rocks will radiate warmth
and the birds will gather there.

Sometimes, a morning squall will chase the sunrise,
clouds massing above the water,
grey and white and dusty blue,
rain drifting along the horizon in stripy veils.

Transubstantiation

The long angle of late June sun
sifts through the trees,
infusing the underbrush
with incandescent light.

It is so very green,
the living essence of green,
that I can smell it,
hear it,
feel the heat of photosynthesis taking place.

I hear the sweet intake of breath and light,
catch the exhale of green atoms
that dance along the luminous evening sunbeams.

Whispers

While we sleep,
draped in sheets silkened
by many washings
and the lightest of summer blankets,
the August evening cools and deepens.

Trees breathe out fresh, cool air
and the grass gives up some of its green.
The breeze whispers through the
screen,
hints of coming fall.

Green Time

In May,
the hourglass up-ends,
an abundance of green
that drips emerald
onto blades of grass,
fills the trees with limey leaves.

Drops
slide through the narrows.
Seconds pass.

The cool nights of early June,
the long stretch of sunlight in July
are suffused with green—
rich and full of promise.

August breathes in the green,
exhales heat and damp,
leaving the grass on the roadside
dry and yellow,
the first fallen leaves brittle
and brown at the edges.

Bouquet – Dismantled

Walking down the pock-marked drive,
I am surprised to see the mullein,
rich creamy white pods just peeking
above the brush.

The lupine has subsided;
the Joe pye weed has gone from
tight purple buds
to frothy lavender feathers.

Wild aster – white – brushes
goldenrod,
tansy shows yellow far into the field.
Daisies peek out cautiously
from the edges.

But it us the mullein that startles me,
reminds me that
August is here.

Tipping Point

For this handful of days,
summer lingers,
suspended like the mid-August sun
that sits on the tips of pines
at the western edge of the field.

Dust motes ride waves of heat,
rising up, up
to dance golden in the light.

For this handful of days,
summer is weightless,
soft and fragranced with new-mown grass.

Dog Days, I

I walk softly through warm, moist air
that rushes into my mouth, nose, lungs,
begins germinating a small seed
of discontent, of longing, inside.

My bare feet can't slide across the linoleum;
the damp bonds them
together like glue.
My skin is tacky, my hair limp.
I am tired and crave
the bitter slap of strong, black coffee.
Late night rains pound their way into my dreams,
green the grass and cool the rooms.

Discontent and longing grow.

Dog Days, II

Trees are sighing in the rainy August night –
not the violent ecstasy of spring winds
pushing through branches
or the caress
of July's hot breath –
but a pent-up sigh of the middle-aged,
tired and still unsatisfied,
afraid of winter.

Dog Days, III

The open window of my car
pulls in the August night
and tosses it about.

The breeze carries all the heat of summer,
the scent of trees exhaling
and the promise of the coming autumn chill.

It is sensuous and weighty,
like a heavy silk.
I wear it all night long.

A Chapel on a Lake

Pouring through the colored glass,
sunlight washes across the floor
in a swath of muddled color.

She stands to the side, sweetly,
calmly. She has no need to move
her pretty hands,
or tilt her open face
in greeting. There is welcome enough.

Around me, fish swim in shards of blue.
The soft breath of a morning breeze
eases around the windows.
I am stunned, brought to sudden tears. There is peace,
there is peace enough.

To the Place Where the Wild Rice Grows

Cutting through high prairie
heading north at 45 degrees,
I saw clouds drop
spoonsful of whipped cream
from the blue-black edge of a front.

A pale orange cat sat on a wooden fencepost
and washed its face,
head cocked.

Clouds strung below the front—
fluffy beads,
tipped by pale golden light.

An egret, white and silent
in a glassy pond,
waiting. Waiting. Waiting.

Behind the clouds, a pink veil
hid the slow retiring sun
of a June evening.

A dappled grey horse
leaned into the deeply corrugated metal
of a pole barn.

The high clouds swirled and parted;
the northern edge of the front dissolved. At the center,
blue light poured through.

Two blackbirds skimmed and swooped
and landed on the tall, thin grass,
the red spots on their wings
a quick glimmer of color.

At the top of the prairie,
I was surrounded by clouds—
to the west, glowing pale yellow and pink,
to the south, the steadfastness of the stubborn black front,
to the east, scattered rain storms forming
purple columns holding up the sky,
to the north, an endless light across the impossibly green grass.

This is what I saw
cutting through the high prairie
to the place where the wild rice grows.

Papa's Garden

I push the seeds of pole beans into tilled earth,
the crust dry and red,
a remnant of clay he's worked 30 years to amend.
They will create a bower along supports
and yield a harvest prolific.
He will stay to eat them all,
fresh and frozen.

The corn in wide-spaced rows
will satisfy his need for size—
tall and green and full of silky ears.
He will pull ripe ears down
from stalks that will tower over his hunched back.
He will be here to pick the corn.

He will pull tomatoes from the vine
still too green for my taste
and leave them to ripen on windowsills
and newsprint wrappers—
safe from marauding raccoons.
He will be eating his tomatoes in October,
maybe November.

If I blanket them with thick mulch,
root vegetables—carrots, beets, rutabagas—
can last all winter long.

But I am counting on the pumpkin,
slow-growing.
Picked mid-fall,
he will eat them in my mother's pies
at Thanksgiving
and at Christmas.

Transitions and Light

.

Transitions and Light

All week the sky has carved itself out
from a shell—
mottled, glorious light
chased by low-hanging clouds.

The sky presses down on trees,
forcing the leaves to the ground,
red with exertion.

My walk is buoyant through
these leaves,
under the mother of pearl sky.

Testament

For weeks, the trees have been breathing
their last.
Aspen tremble at the edge of the field,
their final thoughts gold coins
that flutter and
drift down
into piles of dry riches.

Birch reach up skinny black arms,
graze a clear blue October sky,
their powder-white bodies
stark, naked.

Showy maples shout red, orange, yellow –
loud words
that echo in memory.

Ghosts of tamarack whisper
pale gold promises
of new life,
rebirth.

An eagle perches atop a dying fir,
above the noise,
waiting for a scurrying vole.

Migration

The winds shifted overnight,
torrents of rain
washing leaves from trees.
They lie sodden in muddy grass.
The plums, so ripe, fell like raindrops.

I picked those still hanging on,
prickly branches,
bruised thumbs of purple and red.

And then the high-bush cranberries,
outrageously red,
glowing.
Next the crabapples and their wet leaves.

I wonder at my compulsion
to pick,
to put up,
to capture the sweet juice in jars
that will glow like jewels in the light.

Above me,
a few geese head south.

Aspen

The wind sighs through
the yellowing of late-August
aspen leaves.
They jingle like thin paper coins
as they cling to their branches.

By October, they have become
a rain of gold
against a stark blue sky.

The dry grasses are blanketed
with their extravagance
and airborne coins
dance before our eyes.

A Skim of Ice on Still Water

Slight glaze,
a crystallized wrinkle.
A fine web of tiny cracks
visible only with a half-glance.

The ice doesn't so much distort
as it softens.
It doesn't obscure; it
catches tiny pieces, bits of images.

Life captured in a handful
of frozen molecules gathering
atop a roadside ditch
is vague,
disjointed,
deeply real.

The thin ice throws back
only the rarest of images.

Contrition

Their necks are bent in graceful arch,
heads back,
vulnerable.

The dead deer along the roadside—
ever apologetic—
seek forgiveness,
begging to be excused for getting in the way.

They are sorry for the graceful lines
their bodies make in death. Sorry, too,
that we are saddened to see them.

Forgive us. Forgive us. They plead.
Let us offer up
our necks
so we can be sacrificed
again.

The Shear Zone

The rocks hang.
Jagged,
grieving pieces
lie in tumbles below.
Tiny fault lines are triumphant,
having waited for the right moment
to challenge the certainty,
the wholeness.

I catch the cinnamon of dying leaves,
am reminded of nature's circle
and I think about love
in the shear zone.

Angle of Repose: The Rocks' Reply

We are littered on the hillside,
tumbling down until we rest,
side by side.

We lie where we have fallen,
tossed about by time and life,
circumstance.

Cemeteries on Prairie Roads

In the rich, black earth
they laid them down,
the only trees for acres
casting cool shadows
among modest stones.

They left cavernous red barns
and enduring white clapboard
to walk among rolling fields
of corn and beans and wheat.

They left their labors, for a time,
gathering at a corner church
and walking with a neighbor
who wouldn't return to finish the chores.

In the rich, black earth
they dug the holes.
They planted seeds,
marking years by the rain that fell.

Spring planting, fall harvesting,
winter winds that stripped fields bare
and scattered the rich black earth,
pushing it into etched letters
on stones scattered in groves of trees.

November Skies

Too early, the heavy skies of November are here,
slung low over leafless treetops
that stand on tiptoe,
reaching, reaching
to hold them up.

Their weight oppresses,
deadens color,
flattens the clock
so morning is grey and afternoon is dusk.
The field grass likes matted, supine
from the burden.

Dense and thick,
they buckle under their own weight,
creating long rifts
where the pure blue of October
darts through, shining and hopeful;
it's been here all along.
It's been here all along.

In November, in the Townships

In November
in the townships,
hunters trudge through
brush and wetlands.
Gun shots echo
in the damp fields.
We are quiet
for a moment.

In November,
in the townships,
grass is matted,
gray and ugly.
Skies are leaden,
snowflakes whisper
indistinctly,
softly, softly.

In November
in the townships,
dark falls early,
thick and heavy.
Lights gleam gold from
kitchen windows,
beacons shining
through bare tree limbs.

In November
in the townships,
clear skies shimmer
with bright starlight
shining down on
thin, cold evenings,
and we know that
winter's coming.

Epitaph

The trees exhale—
puffs of color.

Yellow aspen clouds,
dark green firs,
huffing maples with red cheeks.

Sunlight illuminates
their last words,
dying breaths,
their final concessions to winter.

Revelations, Questions

First, the frost.
Rime settles on stringy vines
and colored leaves.
Cell walls swell to bursting
under a thin layer of white.

Then, the North wind
spits and howls and keens
for days and nights on end,
ragged and inconsolable.

What's revealed are pumpkins,
lying plump and orange in the brown field
and the pale-breasted hawk
perched on a naked branch.

What is revealed
when the heart swells
to bursting?
What is stripped away when it keens
and howls and calls
into a deaf and callous night?

Fall on the Prairie

I chased a hidden sun
west across the farmlands of Minnesota,
through Dassel and Montrose,
DeGraff and Waverly.
It glinted briefly on silvery grain elevators
wedged between railroad tracks and two lane;
it hid its face from For Sale signs,
notices of auctions,
peeling paint on the Lutheran church.

The clouds pressed down as I passed
the huge John Deere, a swath of green
that spread across the road
and didn't make apologies for coming home slowly
at the end of a long harvest.

Dark fields undulated on either side,
small clusters of trees held a hill,
guarded a farm house.

Near dusk, the sun dropped below the clouds,
hung low enough for me to touch.

But I had not won.

The hot pink and orange rays shot up
from the end of earth,
sprayed the clouds with color
and painted the thin ice
on a drainage ditch
that twisted through the black, black earth.

Sign

There has been a hard frost.
The grass in the field
is white,
twinkling in the first rays
of a rising sun.

The petunia petals are hard
and brittle—
preserved momentarily
by tiny ice crystals
swelling cells.

Tomorrow, they will hang
limp and brown.
The leaves will fall.
Winter will come.

The Beginning of the Ice

The Beginning of the Ice

In this first cold
snap,
with its achingly clear blue sky
and air thinned to a sharp edge,
the Lake is giving up the last of summer's heat.

Hordes of misty arms
wave in surrender
above its dead surface –
sending clouds
into the dome
of a demanding sky.

It is early January.
Soon the battle will be over,
the arms stilled
beneath a suffocating blanket
of thick, grey ice.

December Skies

Days shorten, darken. Dusk falls
gently in mid afternoon
and eases into a dense black
that settles by suppertime.

December skies are dark, broad, endless,
dotted by stars on the chilliest nights
or blanketed by clouds
that muffle even the thin, white light of the moon.

The nights go on,
almost forever,
but in-between, the colors dance.

Outrageous sunrise shouts pink and orange to the morning!
Sunset works under a pale turquoise sky,
gathering all the colors of the day,
letting them simmer quietly
just above the western treetops.

Grace

Long, pale winter shadows
prostrate themselves before a dying sun.
Snow steals color;
here and there black and white but mostly
too wide an array of grays.

Color startles and warms. The pink
of a child's cheek,
the green of the fir in the thinnest of lights,
comfort.

The night is full of cold sounds –
the wind slapping at windows,
the house groaning,
the rush of snow falling off the roof.

But the clean night sky shyly dances
and glitters.
Evening snows glow with the moon.

Patty's Birthday in Two Parts
for Patty Burke

Morning

The thin air shimmers with light.
The morning sun peeks above the eastern trees,
glowing pale yellow through the pines.

The cold is sharp as a knife,
cutting. Breathing it in hurts.

But, oh! That light.

Night

The moon breathes out
silvery blue light
that glances off
snowy hills and fields
and makes darker the darkened barns
and milk houses.

Cool light
casts insubstantial shadows
in the clear January night.

The nimbus, a pale echo,
fills the sky
and the moon sits in the middle,
glowing with the exertion of each white breath.

These Mornings

The flattened egg yolk of the rising sun,
sits opaque
on the pale blue plate of the horizon.

Cold winter mornings too rarely begin this way –
with icy, bold assurances of life.

More often, they're a monochromatic
scheme of pale greys, white and black;
colorblindness caught
overnight.

But this day dawns cold and clear,
colors ongoing, radiating – no greys
dilute them.

It is for these mornings and their
bold assurances that we awake.

Promises, Green and White

Around an easy corner,
all of a sudden, the land cups
into a gently sloping bowl,
filled with new snow
and evenly dotted with adolescent pines.

The rows run straight and then diagonally
then straight as we pass,
the green almost black in the sunless afternoon.

Arlington.

It looks like a negative
of Arlington, where rows of white
crosses, stark against the greenest of grass,
shift from diagonal to straight to
diagonal when we pass.

The end of so much promise.

Here, where hills slip slowly down
to Lake Superior,
the promises made green and white
are many.

Winter

In the winter,
in the dark,
the black holes of loss
grow deeper,
wider,
more dense.

They gather close,
create a vacuum so powerful
it sucks in joy and light
and the daily pleasure
of coffee in the morning.

My heart is heavy with grieving,
my heart is heavy,
as heavy as these black holes
with their silent rumble and roar
that drown out the sound
of hope.

Solstice

My father will wake in the dark,
spend the precious daylight hours
of his 85th birthday
napping,
struggling with the years that have
worn out his heart,
obscured his vision.

The big night sky falls so early,
stars, crisp and bold,
cutting through the thin, cold air.
He will not see them,
though the cold will suck at
his hands and feet.

I buy him presents,
warm and heavy things
of wool and wood.
To warm him.
To weigh him down
so he cannot float away from me
into the big night sky.

The Field

Paw prints dance like quilt stitches
across the downy white of the field.
Coyote, rabbit, mouse, wolf, deer,
the tracks map out the steps
of a winter *pas de deux*
best danced alone.

The history of the field multiplies daily,
folds onto itself –
        Thursday's coyote seeking
        Wednesday's rabbit,
        the deer leaping over
        day-old wolf tracks,
        giddy in its relief.

January Thaw, I

The cold advances slowly this year,
steady progress halted by too-warm winds,
outrageously warm sunlight.

But in the north, its pace is more certain;
measured draws toward zero.
Ice fingers lace around rocks in the creek.
The cold sucks away the fullness of the
air. It is piercing and crisp,
sharp needles you inhale.

The buff fields wear a dog's thick,
uneven winter coat
and wait for snow.

January Thaw, II

The wind comes from the southwest,
warm, moist
exhaling fog.

It inhales all color;
the world is a monochrome
of grays.

The day is almost languid;
the snow begins melting before dawn.

But it is January;
this will not last.

February at Sugar Lake

You see the pale, pink remainders
of the setting sun
through a filigree of pine boughs
and thin, naked branches.

Car lights move in from the west,
improbably moving
across the white expanse
that is the lake.

A dog barks on the southern shore.
The words of ice fishermen
are clear and distinct.
They are looking for the bucket.

Night is coming.

Life, from the Hillside

From the hillside
the Lake shows tracings of winter –
fingers of ice,
floating bits glinting in the sun,
packs divided by thick snakes of water.

They shift, dissolve,
combine in the easy tide

A tiny stream of snowmelt
inches down the hill.

Rivulets glint in meager
February sunlight
that I thought offered no warmth.

It is enough,
enough to pull molecules of water from the snow,
call them up,
march them down
to the Lake.

Their progress
blocked for a time
by piles of grit and dirt.

This is life.
Slow progress,
temporary delays,
relentless movement.

Woman of the Pines

I am a woman of the pines –
Norway, white and
scraggly Jack.

I am a woman of cool nights
and mornings filled to overflowing
with bird song and the resinous tang of trees.

I am a woman of icy evenings
when freezing pitch swells
and cracks loud
into a clear black sky.

I am a woman of the pines.

The Bath

Last night I washed winter from my body
with too-hot water
and lots of green soap.

In a quiet house,
in a quiet house
I lay in the smooth, white tub
filled with the gurgling
of hot water that
lapped at my belly,
my thighs.

It seeped into me.

And I scrubbed until my skin
was pink and new and smelled of green soap.

But there is no water hot enough
to warm me.

I'm as desolate as a windswept field,
hard as frozen earth.

Bookends

The bookends
of this short December day
hold fast the many promises of light.

Late sunrise is a boisterous orange affair,
careless of the quiet, grey-white world
that blushes pink then peach to think
of such wild, exuberant excess.

By high morning, shard-like glints of light
bounce randomly off crystals in the snow,
the fleeting beauty – cold and pure –
pierces the eye, then penetrates the heart.

This tilted land lifts up its frozen face
for a benediction from a fast-receding sun,
now grown aloof, taking of its leave.

The western trees hold up a parting glance
of richest purple abundance
until the light condenses and bears down,
slips over the edge of the darkened world.

Winter Etching

A feathered brush
of wingtip on snow,
cast blue by late afternoon sun,
punctuates
the flurry
of the rabbit's last steps.

Late Afternoon Walk

Air, honed into a thousand painful edges
under a cold January sky,
cuts into the soft and tender skin
of my neck, my wrists, temples.

I inhale sharp cold
and exhale billows of steam.

My eyes tear
and freeze my eyelashes together.

I revel in the sharp moment,
take in the stunning purple sunset
offered in apology.

Ready

I am anxious for the heavy nights
of December
that fall so completely,
so resolutely,
to be over.

Only January,
And I yearn for the pale aqua mornings
that signal longer days,
melting snow.

Sun and Moon: March

Late afternoon
and the timid March sun
surrenders thin, weak light –
scattering blue, insubstantial shadows on the snow,
offering no warmth.

It slips quietly behind the trees
so as not to offend.

The big moon
rises too quickly,
pure and round and shiny white.
Its shadows are long and deep and strong.
Black.

It rules in absolutes.

Then and Now

Real

Named by a Norwegian immigrant
lonesome for home,
Ugstad Road implies no idyllic landscapes
like, say, Meadowgreen Glade. It tells
straight out about the swamps,
the thin soil, the plenty of rocks.

Ugstad Road has no need to offer false promise
of living things. Unlike Deerfield Acres,
it is thick with deer, with moose, bear,
fox, wolves, rabbits, chipmunks, woodchucks,
raccoons, squirrels, skunks, porcupines,
gophers, cougars, moles and voles.

A priest drove Ugstad Road to perform
last rites; the bank took a home that was built by hand.
Dogs have been killed by speeding cars,
neighbors have pulled each other out of snowy ditches.
The school bus lumbers up and down,
two times every day, and the driver always waves.

On Ugstad Road, the sump pump cycles
through the night each spring,
the peepers offer up a chorus at each dusk,
the mosquitoes find the only hole in the screen
and the Balm-o-Gilead exhales its healing breath
all through the night.

Thresholds/Crossings/Doors

I sort what we will move with us,
what will be thrown,
what will be given away.
I put things into boxes,
into black plastic bags.

I sift through the memories of 17 years –
our granddaughter's first lost tooth,
the dog chasing deer through the field,
the Christmas Eve storm that threatened the party.

I think about who has come through the door,
our north-facing, blue door.
Who has crossed the threshold
of our old farmhouse,
eaten at our table,
sipped a glass of wine.

Papa loved it here; his face lit up
as he came through the door.
He will not cross the threshold
of our new house on the river.

He's opened a different door,
crossed a different threshold,
like Libby, like Elliott, like Robin, like Jackson.

They're not coming with us;
they won't make the move.
There won't be a box
with their names on the label.

I feel I've betrayed them,
left their spirits to wander
from room to room, wondering
where we have gone.

Acknowledgement and Appreciation

I will be forever grateful for the consistent encouragement of my dear friend and colleague, the poet Victor Klimoski, who finally convinced me I could claim the name of poet.

Thank you.

37174777R00042

Made in the USA
Lexington, KY
21 November 2014

Ann Glumac and her husband, Bill Ulland, live on the St. Louis River in Duluth, Minnesota, where she is a consultant and trainer.

This, her first book of poetry, contains observations and reflections about the natural world, the changing of seasons, the seasons of life.

ISBN 9781469907673

90000 >

9 781469 907673